MERCEDES-BENZ

Jill C. Wheeler

ABDO
& Daughters

VISIT US AT
WWW.ABDOPUB.COM

Published by ABDO Publishing Company, 4940 Viking Drive, Suite 622, Edina, Minnesota 55435. Copyright ©2004 by Abdo Consulting Group, Inc. International copyrights reserved in all countries. No part of this book may be reproduced in any form without written permission from the publisher.

Printed in the United States.

Edited by: Katharine Thorbeck
Contributing Editor: Alan Pierce
Interior Production and Design: Terry Dunham Incorporated
Cover Design: Mighty Media
Photos: Corbis, Ron Kimball Photography

Library of Congress Cataloging-in-Publication Data

Wheeler, Jill C., 1964-
  Mercedes-Benz / Jill C. Wheeler.
    p. cm. -- (Ultimate Cars)
  Includes index.
  ISBN 1-59197-581-6
  1. Mercedes automobile--History--Juvenile literature. [1. Mercedes automobile--History.] I. Title. II. Series.

TL215.M18W44 2004
629.222'2--dc22

                                  2003063804

Contents

The Original Automobile

If you asked who makes the world's best car, many people would tell you it is Mercedes-Benz. Mercedes-Benz, sometimes just called Mercedes, is the top brand of DaimlerChrysler AG. The Mercedes name symbolizes luxury, quality engineering, and the pure joy of driving. Its famous three-pointed star is one of the world's best known trademarks.

Mercedes-Benz can be traced back to two men, Gottlieb Daimler and Carl Benz. Strangely, Daimler and Benz never met. They worked independently to create the first automobile engine. They were each unaware of the other's efforts. Now, their names are forever linked in history as the pioneers of one of the world's finest cars.

Mercedes-Benz automobiles have been setting standards in racing, handling, safety, and reliability since the early 1900s. Company engineers have invented many of today's standard automotive technologies. For example, anti-lock brakes, airbags, and crumple zones all first appeared on Mercedes-Benz cars.

The First Cars

The motorcar has its roots in the work of two German engineers. In the late 1800s, Gottlieb Daimler and Carl Benz both dreamed of making a "horseless carriage." In those days, people used carriages drawn by horses to get around. Daimler and Benz thought it was time to invent something more efficient. The first challenge was finding the right engine.

Most engines of the time were powered by steam. They were large, slow, and heavy. Daimler was convinced the "horseless carriage" needed something different. So he used his engineering skills to work on an internal combustion engine that was suitable for a vehicle. He had seen Etienne Lenoir's simple, stationary version of the engine on a visit to Paris, France. He was determined to put it on wheels and perfect it.

Carl Benz is credited with building the first car powered by an internal combustion engine.

Gottlieb Daimler helped develop the gas-powered engine that could be used for motorcars.

Daimler eventually quit his engineering job at Deutz Gas Motor Works. He set up a workshop in the backyard of his home in Cannstatt, Germany. He and fellow engineer Wilhelm Maybach labored from dawn to midnight for about a year. Finally, they reached their goal. They created a high-speed, lightweight, gasoline-powered engine. Daimler patented the new engine in December 1883.

Daimler first put his engine on a bicycle design in 1885. It became the world's first motorcycle. He didn't pursue making motorcycles because he wanted to build a bigger vehicle for families to use. Although Daimler and Maybach focused on cars, their engine soon powered boats, trolley cars, airships, and even trains.

Daimler and Maybach kept improving on their creations. They created a steel wheel car in 1889. It was a true vehicle, not just a modified carriage. Their earlier designs were built from a carriage model, but without the drawbar for the horses. The "wire wheel" car featured a twin-cylinder V-type engine and four gears.

Meanwhile, some 60 miles (96 km) away in Mannheim, Germany, Carl Benz was also working on a "horseless carriage." Benz, like Daimler, was a skilled engineer. He developed a gasoline-powered engine, too. Then he worked with bicycle mechanics to put it on a three-wheeled vehicle. The vehicle could travel at speeds of up to 10 miles per hour (16 km/h). Benz patented his vehicle in January 1886. His three-wheeled *Patent-Motorwagen* is considered the world's first car.

Both men began selling their hand-built vehicles. Most people thought these new vehicles were strange and a bit frightening. Clearly, the auto market needed a push.

Carl Benz's wife, Bertha, helped do just that. One day in August 1888, she had to make a 54-mile (88 km) trip to her hometown, Pforzheim. Bertha gathered her two boys, Eugen and Richard, and piled them into the *Patent-Motorwagen*. Although the car struggled to get up hills, Bertha and the boys reached their destination safely. This famous journey helped prove the safety of the new motorcar.

The 1886 Benz Patent-Motorwagen was promoted as an alternative to the horse and carriage. However, it took awhile for the public to welcome the strange, new machine.

Fast Start

Benz and Daimler each started a company. Benz's company became known as Benz & Cie. It was the world's largest manufacturer of automobiles by 1899. In 1890, Daimler started Daimler Motoren-Gesellschaft, A.G. (DMG). Later, the company used an emblem with three stars. The stars stood for land, air, and water. Daimler's engines had powered machines that traveled all three.

Daimler died in March 1900. Sadly, he did not live to see the growth of his company. An Austrian businessman named Emil Jellinek stepped in and took over Daimler's vision. Jellinek had bought one of the first Daimler cars in 1897. He raced it in the "Tour de Nice" in Nice, France and won. He liked the car so much that he bought 36 more on the condition that DMG would make cars to his liking.

Jellinek had big ideas for the new cars. He convinced Daimler's son, Paul, and Wilhelm Maybach to make faster, more stylish vehicles. He also wanted to change the company name from Daimler to Mercedes. Mercedes was his 10-year-old daughter's name.

The first Mercedes car was delivered to Jellinek in December 1900. The feisty Austrian got his wish for a fast, stylish car. Maybach designed the Mercedes 35 horsepower (hp) with a low center of gravity, a pressed-steel frame, and four speeds including reverse. Its top speed was 47 mph (76 km/h). A new era of speed and performance in automotive history had begun.

In 1908, workers paint a car at the Daimler Motor factory in Germany.

The new Mercedes cars gobbled the lion's share of the auto market. Until the Mercedes arrived, Benz & Cie was the biggest automotive manufacturer around. In 1900, Benz had sold 603 cars. But by 1903, Benz's sales had slipped to 172. DMG and Benz were suddenly rival companies. Benz executives knew they had to do something to compete. Some suggested the company make faster cars.

But, Carl Benz disagreed. He did not see why any car should go faster than 30 mph (48 km/h). The board of directors overruled Benz, however, and he resigned in 1903. For all his brilliance, Benz couldn't understand people's desire for speed.

Benz & Cie then began to design faster cars. Benz later changed his mind about the appeal of speed and rejoined his company in 1904. He watched as the "Blitzen Benz," a bullet-shaped car, set a new land speed record in 1909. *Blitzen* means lightning in German. The lightning-quick roadster hit 141 mph (227 km/h) to set a record that remained unbroken for 15 years.

DMG and Benz & Cie had become powerhouses by the start of World War I in 1914. German officials asked both car companies to help Germany win the war. DMG and Benz began producing airplane engines.

World War I severely damaged the German economy. Few people had money to buy cars after the war. DMG and Benz struggled to sell their quality products. Because of such

hard times, the rival companies decided to merge. So, Daimler Motoren-Gesellschaft and Benz & Cie became Daimler-Benz A.G. in 1926. They decided to call their cars Mercedes-Benz.

American driver Bob Burman is shown here with a Blitzen Benz in 1914.

The K and S Series

The new company looked to the talented Dr. Ferdinand Porsche for a new line. They didn't have to look far, because Porsche was the chief engineer at DMG. During his short time at Daimler-Benz, he designed cars that used something Paul Daimler had been developing. It was called a supercharger. The supercharger could instantly boost an engine's horsepower.

Porsche put the supercharger in the first new Mercedes-Benz design. It was the Model K for *kurz*, which means short in German. The Model K chassis was smaller and lighter than the chassis used in earlier cars. It was used in two series, the 500K and the 540K. Daimler-Benz only provided the chassis of the K cars. Coachbuilders provided the sleek bodies and details. This process was common at the time.

The 500K could exceed 100 mph (160 km/h). The 540K, when supercharged, had 180 hp. It was one of the most powerful cars of the time. But the 540K had more than just power. *Motor Sport* magazine gushed that the car could do "a gliding crawl in absolute silence." So it was both speedy and smooth.

The 1930s

Daimler-Benz continued to grow throughout the 1930s. However, worldwide, the automobile industry was suffering because of the Great Depression. In 1929, the year the Depression began, the United States produced 5.3 million automobiles. By 1930, the United States made fewer than 2.4 million cars. Eight years later, U.S. car manufacturers made 2.5 million cars. When World War II began Daimler-Benz and American car makers switched to making military equipment.

The Mercedes-Benz 540K was big, fast, and powerful. But the car was also expensive.

The 500K and 540K series were top-of-the-line for Daimler-Benz. They were status symbols among the wealthy. The company also produced the more affordable 290, 230, and 170 series. The 170 became the company's bestseller in the 1930s. It was about half the price of the K series cars. The 170 still offered a 1.7-liter 6-cylinder engine, a four-wheel independent suspension, and four-wheel hydraulic brakes, but it was mass-produced to make it more affordable. The 170 even had an anti-theft lock on the steering wheel. In 1936, Daimler-Benz introduced the 170V, a 4-cylinder version. The two-seat roadster sold for about $1,250.

Although it was busy producing affordable cars, Daimler-Benz had not lost its passion for speed. It also developed a faster version of the K, called the S, for "sports." The S featured a new drop-center frame that lowered the car's center of gravity. This innovation greatly improved handling. The Super Sport (SS) model appeared in 1928 and featured up to 225 hp when supercharged. It was followed by the SSK for Super Sport *Kurz*.

The Mercedes-Benz S cars became the kings of European racing in the 1920s and 1930s. They were excellent performers because the Mercedes-Benz team did a lot of research to prepare for races. For example, the team scouted the track before the race to memorize every curve. It also rehearsed tire changing and refueling until it did these responsibilities better than any other team.

Daimler-Benz also developed an enormous sedan in the late 1920s. The Type 770, or the Grosser, had a giant 7.7-liter, 8-cylinder supercharged engine. It was designed to be driven by a chauffeur. The Grosser became a favorite of German dictator Adolph Hitler. Grosser sedans were very regal. Even Emperor Hirohito of Japan had one.

Adolph Hitler's Mercedes-Benz car in the 1930s.

Racing to Glory

Adolph Hitler liked Mercedes-Benz sedans. He also loved race cars. Hitler asked Daimler-Benz to build a Grand Prix car to show off German engineering talent. The result was the W 25. It featured a supercharged engine with 400 hp. The W 25 began its racing career in the summer of 1934. It won five races and set a world record for speed. The W 25 averaged 117.19 mph (189 km/h).

In 1935, Mercedes-Benz cars won nine out of ten races, including six Grand Prix events.

Then in 1937, Mercedes-Benz hit the track with a car like no other. It introduced the W 125. The W 125 weighed the same as the W 25, but it had nearly twice as much horsepower. The W 125 helped Mercedes-Benz dominate racing in the 1930s. Between 1934 and 1939, the car finished first 34 times. The Auto Union team came in first just 11 times. The Mercedes-Benz victories came from not only a superior car. They also came from a well-equipped and well-rehearsed racing team.

The W 125 set a record on the German *autobahn* in 1938. It reached a speed of 271 mph (433 km/h). But even that was not fast enough for Daimler-Benz. The company set a new goal to build the world's fastest car. They called the project T80.

Engineers selected a 12-cylinder airplane engine for the T80. The 44.5-liter engine was rated at 2800 hp. It had an estimated top speed of 406 mph (650 km/h). But, World War II began one month before the car was to be finished. Unfortunately, the T80 was never raced.

German drivers work on their Mercedes-Benz race cars in 1937. The drivers are preparing for the International Donnington Grand Prix in England.

Rebuilding a Giant

World War II stopped car production in Germany. Daimler-Benz factories began building engines for tanks, bombers, and fighter planes, instead. They also built trucks and other military vehicles for the German government. Some of this work was done with forced laborers from concentration camps.

Daimler-Benz built even better airplane engines than the separate companies, DMG and Benz & Cie., had during World War I. They produced the supercharged DB-600 series V-12 engine for the famous Messerschmitt Bf-109 fighter plane. The engine was actually mounted upside down to better fit the aircraft design. Its power became legendary.

Building military equipment made Daimler-Benz factories targets for Allied bombers. There was little left of the company when the war ended. The once giant Daimler-Benz was reduced to shambles, just like the rest of defeated Germany.

Eventually, Daimler-Benz began producing cars again. The company built just over 200 cars in 1947. The first model was the 170 V, followed by the 170 S and 170 D. Output of these touring sedans grew to around 50,000 cars per year by the early 1950s.

The first all-new post-war models, the 220 and 300, were introduced in 1951. These six-cylinder cars helped ease

Daimler-Benz back into its position as a leading luxury carmaker. The 300 was the largest and fastest German production car of the time. It was later the basis for the modern Mercedes-Benz S Class car.

During the early 1950s, the company was gaining strength with its passenger cars. But, it was time to get back to racing. In 1952, Mercedes introduced the 300 SL coupe. The coupe featured a six-cylinder, 3.0-liter engine that delivered 173 hp. It had sleek gullwing doors and a removable steering wheel.

The 1955 Mercedes-Benz
300 SL Gullwing Coupe

Daimler-Benz made just 1,400 cars with gullwing doors before changing to a conventional door design. Many people were sad about the change because they loved the elegant and unusual look of the seagull-inspired doors.

The 300 SL gullwing coupe turned in a respectable racing performance. It won in Le Mans, France, and at the German Grand Prix. A later version of the coupe, the 300 SLR, was the first car to use an air brake system. This was a large metal flap behind the seat that helped slow the car. Drivers soon realized that when the flap was open, the wheels hugged the ground. This is how Mercedes-Benz engineers accidentally discovered ground effects. Ground effects wings, now common features, help race cars stay on track.

Daimler-Benz adapted the 300 SL coupe for non-racers in 1954. It became very popular among movie stars and sports car buffs. The car had a top speed of 155 mph (248 km/h). The 300 SL remains one of the most famous Mercedes-Benz models ever made.

In 1955, a tragedy caused Mercedes-Benz to retire from racing. Mercedes driver Pierre Levegh was racing a 300 SLR at the Le Mans race. Suddenly, a slower car pulled in front of him. Levegh swerved to avoid hitting the other car, but they collided anyway. The SLR was flung into a crowd of spectators. Levegh and more than 80 racing fans died.

A 1954 Mercedes-Benz race car

A Return to Racing

Mercedes-Benz sat on the racing sidelines until the late 1980s. Meanwhile its competitors, such as BMW and Jaguar, were tearing up the track. The competitors were calling attention to themselves. Mercedes' absence was felt.

Mercedes finally returned to the racetrack with the help of Peter Sauber. Sauber was a wealthy Swiss race car designer. Sauber wanted to use Mercedes engines in the cars he designed. This was a good deal for both Sauber and Mercedes.

The Sauber-Mercedes cars began to appear in the World Sports Car Championship series. They featured the powerful twin-turbocharged, 5.0-liter V-8 engines that had been in Mercedes-Benz sedans. The engines had more than 700 hp by the time Sauber's team finished tweaking them. The cars also used the ground effects that Mercedes-Benz drivers and engineers had discovered in the 1950s.

In 1988, Daimler-Benz formally announced that it was back in racing. Sauber-Mercedes cars won in Germany and Belgium, but they lost in Le Mans. The Mercedes-Benz team did not always walk away with top honors. But, its experiences on the track helped it revive a tradition of innovation and quality engineering.

In typical Mercedes style, the racing team kept working hard. In 1998, the Mercedes-Benz team had an extremely successful year. The team earned 21 victories in 45 races. It even won the Formula One World Championship.

Today, Mercedes-Benz cars can be found in the German Touring Car Masters (DTM) series. They also continue to race in the Formula One and Formula Three racing series. In 1995, Mercedes-Benz joined McLaren, a prestigious race team, to become its engine partner. They are called Team McLaren Mercedes.

In 2000, Mika Hakkinen of Finland races for McLaren Mercedes at the European Grand Prix in Germany.

Modern Mercedes

Mercedes-Benz has been a household name for more than 50 years. However, in another significant union, Daimler-Benz merged with U.S.-based Chrysler Corporation in 1998. The merged company is now called DaimlerChrysler AG. The Mercedes-Benz brand name remains the same, and it still uses the revered three-star emblem.

There have been so many models and classes of Mercedes-Benz cars that it's hard to keep them all straight! The cars are all named from a coding system. Most models feature three numbers followed by two or three letters. The numbers indicate the size of the engine. A 500 model means the car has a 5.0-liter engine. Similarly, a 320 model means the car has a 3.2-liter engine.

Mercedes-Benz cars now have five different body styles. There is the sedan, the coupe, the roadster, the wagon, and the sport utility vehicle (SUV). In the United States, the five styles fit into nine classes: they are the C, E, S, CLK, CL, SLK, SL, M, and G. The M and the G classes refer to SUVs, which are popular with today's drivers.

The C Class and the E Class are also popular. By October 2003, DaimlerChrysler AG had sold 55,800 C Class vehicles.

By January 2003, 43,000 E Class had been sold. The more luxurious CLK is also a hot seller in the United States.

Like many classes, the CLK Class has different models with a range of features. For example, the 2004 CLK 320 Coupe has a 3.2-liter, V-6 engine with 215 hp. It sells for about $45,000. The higher-end model, the CLK55 AMG, features a mighty 5.5-liter, V-8 engine that delivers a whopping 362 hp. It's not surprising that the 2004 CLK 55 AMG costs an equally whopping $80,220.

There are several Mercedes even mightier than the CLK55 AMG. One of them is not even available in the United States. It is the Mercedes-Benz SLR McLaren. The car caused quite a stir when it debuted at the Frankfurt International Motor Show (IAA) on September 9, 2003. It has a supercharged V-8 engine and three-shift programs on the five-speed automatic transmission. The SLR McLaren is called "the silver arrow of the twenty-first century."

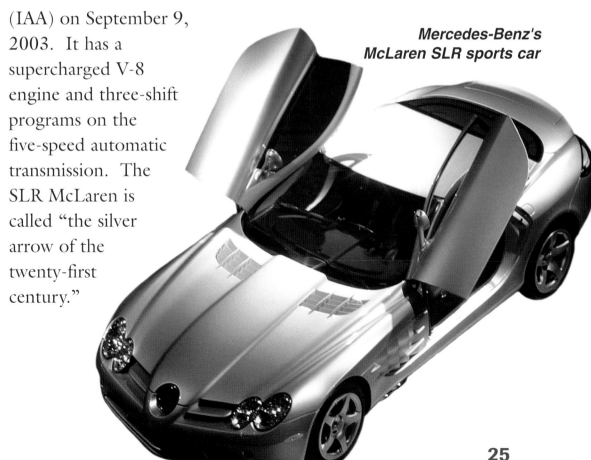

Mercedes-Benz's McLaren SLR sports car

Another Mercedes that is on its way to series production is the Vision CLS Coupe. It first appeared as a concept car at the IAA in 2003. The Vision will be the basis for the new CLS Class. The Vision is a four-door coupe that is both sporty and comfortable. It features a seven-gear automatic transmission and a bi-xenon Active Light System. The Vision CLS Coupe is an example of the kind of car Mercedes-Benz will make in the future.

New Horizons

Most car makers know that making cars for the future means thinking about what's good for the environment. Today, DaimlerChrysler is working on cars powered by fuel cells. Fuel cells are a source of electricity. They are good for the environment because they power engines by a chemical reaction of hydrogen and oxygen instead of by burning fuel. The fuel cell engine produces less pollution (in some cases none) than the conventional internal combustion method.

Mercedes-Benz produced an experimental fuel cell vehicle in 1994. In October 2002, DaimlerChrysler introduced the "F-Cell" A Class fleet. It was the first small-scale series of fuel-cell-powered cars ever made. The A Class looks like a cross between a minivan and an SUV. As of 2003, the fleet is in the process of practical road testing. DaimlerChrysler expects to begin making fuel cell cars available to the public around 2005. Adoption of fuel cell technology will help reduce the world's dependence on fossil fuels such as petroleum.

The future looks bright. Mercedes-Benz keeps the competition busy by pursuing new designs, such as the CLS and

A Classes, and new technologies, such as the bi-xenon Active Light System, and the fuel cell. It's a tough act to follow, both now and then. Starting with Carl Benz's *Patent-Motorwagen* in 1886, Mercedes-Benz always puts something exciting on the road.

2003 Mercedes-Benz SL500

Timeline

1883

Gottlieb Daimler patents his first high-speed gasoline engines.

1886

Carl Benz patents the *Patent-Motorwagen*.

1890

Daimler Motoren-Gesellschaft, A.G. is formed.

1900

Daimler dies.

1901

Daimler Company introduces the Mercedes.

1909

Blitzen Benz race car sets new land speed record.

1914-1918

DMG and Benz & Cie build engines during World War I.

1926

Daimler Motoren-Gesellschaft and Benz & Cie merge, forming Daimler-Benz, A.G.

1938

Mercedes-Benz W 125 sets land speed record
of 271 mph (433 km/h).

1939-1945

Mercedes-Benz redirects efforts toward military production
during World War II.

1952

Mercedes-Benz 300 SL racing car appears.

1955

Mercedes-Benz retires from racing.

1988

Mercedes-Benz returns to racing.

1998

Daimler-Benz merges with the Chrysler Corporation.

2003

Chrysler Group invests $1.4 billion in its Brampton plant in
Canada to produce a new line of sedans. Chrysler Group is the
North American branch of DaimlerChrysler.

Glossary

Allied: the nations that fought against Germany in World War II.

apprentice: someone who learns a trade or craft by working with a skilled person.

autobahn: a German superhighway that often has no speed limit.

carburetor: a device in engines that produces a vapor of gasoline and air for easy burning.

chassis: the frame and mechanical parts of a car, excluding the body.

concentration camp: a walled-off prison area where people were killed, tortured or left to die, or forced to work without pay during World War II.

crumple zone: an area of a car that is designed to buckle during an accident.

dictator: someone who has complete control of a country, often ruling it unjustly.

fuel cell: a device that uses chemical reactions to produce electricity.

ground effects: the shaping of a car body to create a vacuum that "sticks" a race car to the track for better handling.

supercharger: an engine-driven pump that forces gas-air mixture into an engine to generate more power than the engine would normally produce.

Internet Sites

www.abdopub.com

Would you like to learn more about the Mercedes-Benz? Please visit **www.abdopub.com** to find up-to-date Web site links about the Mercedes-Benz and other Ultimate Cars. These links are routinely monitored and updated to provide the most current information available.

Index